Save Time and Money
with a List-based
Meal Planner

@ Journals and Notebooks

@ Journals & Notebooks

To Do List

Breakfast

Lunch

Shopping List

Dinner

Breakfast

- [ ]
- [ ]
- [ ]
- [ ]
- [ ]
- [ ]
- [ ]
- [ ]

Lunch

- [ ]
- [ ]
- [ ]
- [ ]
- [ ]
- [ ]
- [ ]
- [ ]

Dinner

Breakfast

Lunch

Shopping List

Dinner

- [ ]
- [ ]
- [ ]
- [ ]
- [ ]
- [ ]
- [ ]
- [ ]

To Do List

Breakfast

- [ ]
- [ ]
- [ ]
- [ ]
- [ ]
- [ ]
- [ ]
- [ ]

Lunch

- [ ]
- [ ]
- [ ]
- [ ]
- [ ]
- [ ]
- [ ]
- [ ]

Shopping List

Dinner

- [ ]
- [ ]
- [ ]
- [ ]
- [ ]
- [ ]
- [ ]
- [ ]

To Do List

Breakfast

- [ ]
- [ ]
- [ ]
- [ ]
- [ ]
- [ ]
- [ ]
- [ ]

Lunch

- [ ]
- [ ]
- [ ]
- [ ]
- [ ]
- [ ]
- [ ]
- [ ]

Eat
Healthy

Dinner

- [ ]
- [ ]
- [ ]
- [ ]
- [ ]
- [ ]
- [ ]
- [ ]

Breakfast

- [ ]
- [ ]
- [ ]
- [ ]
- [ ]
- [ ]
- [ ]
- [ ]

Lunch

- [ ]
- [ ]
- [ ]
- [ ]
- [ ]
- [ ]
- [ ]
- [ ]

Shopping List

Dinner

- [ ]
- [ ]
- [ ]
- [ ]
- [ ]
- [ ]
- [ ]
- [ ]

<table>
<tr><td>

To Do List

</td><td>

Breakfast

☐ ______________
☐ ______________
☐ ______________
☐ ______________
☐ ______________
☐ ______________
☐ ______________
☐ ______________

</td></tr>
<tr><td></td><td>

Lunch

☐ ______________
☐ ______________
☐ ______________
☐ ______________
☐ ______________
☐ ______________
☐ ______________
☐ ______________

</td></tr>
</table>

Shopping
List

Dinner

Breakfast

Lunch

Shopping List

Dinner

- [ ]
- [ ]
- [ ]
- [ ]
- [ ]
- [ ]
- [ ]
- [ ]

To Do List

Breakfast

Lunch

Shopping List

Dinner

Breakfast

☐ _______________________________
☐ _______________________________
☐ _______________________________
☐ _______________________________
☐ _______________________________
☐ _______________________________
☐ _______________________________
☐ _______________________________

Lunch

☐ _______________________________
☐ _______________________________
☐ _______________________________
☐ _______________________________
☐ _______________________________
☐ _______________________________
☐ _______________________________
☐ _______________________________

Shopping List

Dinner

Breakfast

- [ ]
- [ ]
- [ ]
- [ ]
- [ ]
- [ ]
- [ ]
- [ ]

Lunch

- [ ]
- [ ]
- [ ]
- [ ]
- [ ]
- [ ]
- [ ]
- [ ]

Dinner

To Do List

Breakfast

Lunch

Shopping List

Dinner

- ☐
- ☐
- ☐
- ☐
- ☐
- ☐
- ☐
- ☐

To Do List

Breakfast

Lunch

Shopping List

Dinner

- [ ]
- [ ]
- [ ]
- [ ]
- [ ]
- [ ]
- [ ]
- [ ]

To Do List

Breakfast

- [ ]
- [ ]
- [ ]
- [ ]
- [ ]
- [ ]
- [ ]
- [ ]

Lunch

- [ ]
- [ ]
- [ ]
- [ ]
- [ ]
- [ ]
- [ ]
- [ ]

Shopping
List

Dinner

- [ ]
- [ ]
- [ ]
- [ ]
- [ ]
- [ ]
- [ ]
- [ ]

To Do List

Breakfast

Lunch

Shopping List

____

____

____

____

____

____

____

____

____

____

____

Dinner

- ☐ ________________________
- ☐ ________________________
- ☐ ________________________
- ☐ ________________________
- ☐ ________________________
- ☐ ________________________
- ☐ ________________________
- ☐ ________________________

Breakfast

Lunch

Eat
Healthy

Shopping List

Dinner

Breakfast

- ☐ ____________________
- ☐ ____________________
- ☐ ____________________
- ☐ ____________________
- ☐ ____________________
- ☐ ____________________
- ☐ ____________________
- ☐ ____________________

Lunch

- ☐ ____________________
- ☐ ____________________
- ☐ ____________________
- ☐ ____________________
- ☐ ____________________
- ☐ ____________________
- ☐ ____________________
- ☐ ____________________

Shopping List

Dinner

- [ ]
- [ ]
- [ ]
- [ ]
- [ ]
- [ ]
- [ ]
- [ ]

Breakfast

Lunch

Shopping List

Dinner

- [ ]
- [ ]
- [ ]
- [ ]
- [ ]
- [ ]
- [ ]
- [ ]

To Do List

Breakfast

Lunch

Eat Healthy

Shopping List

Dinner

- [ ]
- [ ]
- [ ]
- [ ]
- [ ]
- [ ]
- [ ]
- [ ]

Breakfast

- [ ]
- [ ]
- [ ]
- [ ]
- [ ]
- [ ]
- [ ]
- [ ]

Lunch

- [ ]
- [ ]
- [ ]
- [ ]
- [ ]
- [ ]
- [ ]
- [ ]

Shopping List

Dinner

- [ ]
- [ ]
- [ ]
- [ ]
- [ ]
- [ ]
- [ ]
- [ ]

To Do List

____

____

____

____

____

____

____

____

____

____

____

____

Breakfast

- ☐ ____________________
- ☐ ____________________
- ☐ ____________________
- ☐ ____________________
- ☐ ____________________
- ☐ ____________________
- ☐ ____________________
- ☐ ____________________

Lunch

- ☐ ____________________
- ☐ ____________________
- ☐ ____________________
- ☐ ____________________
- ☐ ____________________
- ☐ ____________________
- ☐ ____________________
- ☐ ____________________

Dinner

- [ ]
- [ ]
- [ ]
- [ ]
- [ ]
- [ ]
- [ ]
- [ ]

<table>
<tr>
<td>

To Do List

____

____

____

____

____

____

____

____

____

____

____

</td>
<td>

Breakfast

☐ ___________
☐ ___________
☐ ___________
☐ ___________
☐ ___________
☐ ___________
☐ ___________
☐ ___________

Lunch

☐ ___________
☐ ___________
☐ ___________
☐ ___________
☐ ___________
☐ ___________
☐ ___________
☐ ___________

</td>
</tr>
</table>

Shopping List

Dinner

Breakfast

Lunch

Shopping List

Dinner

To Do List

Breakfast

Lunch

Shopping List

Dinner

Breakfast

- [ ]
- [ ]
- [ ]
- [ ]
- [ ]
- [ ]
- [ ]
- [ ]

Lunch

- [ ]
- [ ]
- [ ]
- [ ]
- [ ]
- [ ]
- [ ]
- [ ]

Dinner

- [ ]
- [ ]
- [ ]
- [ ]
- [ ]
- [ ]
- [ ]
- [ ]

To Do List

Breakfast

- [ ]
- [ ]
- [ ]
- [ ]
- [ ]
- [ ]
- [ ]
- [ ]

Lunch

- [ ]
- [ ]
- [ ]
- [ ]
- [ ]
- [ ]
- [ ]
- [ ]

Shopping List

____

____

____

____

____

____

____

____

____

____

____

Dinner

- [ ] ____________________
- [ ] ____________________
- [ ] ____________________
- [ ] ____________________
- [ ] ____________________
- [ ] ____________________
- [ ] ____________________
- [ ] ____________________

To Do List

Breakfast

- [ ]
- [ ]
- [ ]
- [ ]
- [ ]
- [ ]
- [ ]
- [ ]

Lunch

- [ ]
- [ ]
- [ ]
- [ ]
- [ ]
- [ ]
- [ ]
- [ ]

Eat Healthy

Shopping
List

Dinner

Eat
Healthy

To Do List

Breakfast

Lunch

Shopping List

Dinner

- [ ]
- [ ]
- [ ]
- [ ]
- [ ]
- [ ]
- [ ]
- [ ]

To Do List

Breakfast

Lunch

Dinner

- [ ]
- [ ]
- [ ]
- [ ]
- [ ]
- [ ]
- [ ]
- [ ]

Breakfast

Lunch

Shopping List

Dinner

- [ ]
- [ ]
- [ ]
- [ ]
- [ ]
- [ ]
- [ ]
- [ ]

To Do List

Breakfast

Lunch

Dinner

To Do List

Breakfast

Lunch

Shopping List

Dinner

- [ ]
- [ ]
- [ ]
- [ ]
- [ ]
- [ ]
- [ ]
- [ ]

To Do List

Breakfast

Lunch

Dinner

- [ ]
- [ ]
- [ ]
- [ ]
- [ ]
- [ ]
- [ ]
- [ ]

To Do List

Breakfast

- [ ]
- [ ]
- [ ]
- [ ]
- [ ]
- [ ]
- [ ]
- [ ]

Lunch

- [ ]
- [ ]
- [ ]
- [ ]
- [ ]
- [ ]
- [ ]
- [ ]

Shopping List

____

____

____

____

____

____

____

____

____

____

____

____

Dinner

- ☐ _______________
- ☐ _______________
- ☐ _______________
- ☐ _______________
- ☐ _______________
- ☐ _______________
- ☐ _______________
- ☐ _______________

Breakfast

- [ ]
- [ ]
- [ ]
- [ ]
- [ ]
- [ ]
- [ ]
- [ ]

Lunch

- [ ]
- [ ]
- [ ]
- [ ]
- [ ]
- [ ]
- [ ]
- [ ]

Shopping List

Dinner

- [ ] ______________________
- [ ] ______________________
- [ ] ______________________
- [ ] ______________________
- [ ] ______________________
- [ ] ______________________
- [ ] ______________________
- [ ] ______________________

Breakfast

- [ ]
- [ ]
- [ ]
- [ ]
- [ ]
- [ ]
- [ ]
- [ ]

Lunch

- [ ]
- [ ]
- [ ]
- [ ]
- [ ]
- [ ]
- [ ]
- [ ]

Shopping List

Dinner

- [ ]
- [ ]
- [ ]
- [ ]
- [ ]
- [ ]
- [ ]
- [ ]

To Do List

Breakfast

Lunch

Shopping List

Dinner

To Do List

Breakfast

Lunch

Shopping List

____

____

____

____

____

____

____

____

____

____

____

____

Dinner

☐ ____________________

☐ ____________________

☐ ____________________

☐ ____________________

☐ ____________________

☐ ____________________

☐ ____________________

☐ ____________________

Breakfast

Lunch

Eat
Healthy

Shopping List

Dinner

Breakfast

Lunch

Shopping List

Dinner

- [ ]
- [ ]
- [ ]
- [ ]
- [ ]
- [ ]
- [ ]
- [ ]

Breakfast

- [ ]
- [ ]
- [ ]
- [ ]
- [ ]
- [ ]
- [ ]
- [ ]

Lunch

- [ ]
- [ ]
- [ ]
- [ ]
- [ ]
- [ ]
- [ ]
- [ ]

Shopping List

Dinner

Breakfast

☐ _______________________
☐ _______________________
☐ _______________________
☐ _______________________
☐ _______________________
☐ _______________________
☐ _______________________
☐ _______________________

Lunch

☐ _______________________
☐ _______________________
☐ _______________________
☐ _______________________
☐ _______________________
☐ _______________________
☐ _______________________
☐ _______________________

Shopping List

Dinner

To Do List

Breakfast

- [ ]
- [ ]
- [ ]
- [ ]
- [ ]
- [ ]
- [ ]
- [ ]

Lunch

- [ ]
- [ ]
- [ ]
- [ ]
- [ ]
- [ ]
- [ ]
- [ ]

Shopping List

Dinner

To Do List

Breakfast

- ☐
- ☐
- ☐
- ☐
- ☐
- ☐
- ☐
- ☐

Lunch

- ☐
- ☐
- ☐
- ☐
- ☐
- ☐
- ☐
- ☐

Shopping List

Dinner

- [ ]
- [ ]
- [ ]
- [ ]
- [ ]
- [ ]
- [ ]
- [ ]

Breakfast

- [ ]
- [ ]
- [ ]
- [ ]
- [ ]
- [ ]
- [ ]
- [ ]

Lunch

- [ ]
- [ ]
- [ ]
- [ ]
- [ ]
- [ ]
- [ ]
- [ ]

Shopping List

Dinner

- [ ]
- [ ]
- [ ]
- [ ]
- [ ]
- [ ]
- [ ]
- [ ]

Breakfast

Lunch

Shopping List

Dinner

- [ ]
- [ ]
- [ ]
- [ ]
- [ ]
- [ ]
- [ ]
- [ ]

To Do List

Breakfast

☐
☐
☐
☐
☐
☐
☐
☐

Lunch

☐
☐
☐
☐
☐
☐
☐
☐

Shopping List

Dinner

Breakfast

- [ ]
- [ ]
- [ ]
- [ ]
- [ ]
- [ ]
- [ ]
- [ ]

Lunch

- [ ]
- [ ]
- [ ]
- [ ]
- [ ]
- [ ]
- [ ]
- [ ]

Dinner

To Do List

Breakfast

- [ ]
- [ ]
- [ ]
- [ ]
- [ ]
- [ ]
- [ ]
- [ ]

Lunch

- [ ]
- [ ]
- [ ]
- [ ]
- [ ]
- [ ]
- [ ]
- [ ]

Eat Healthy

Dinner

Eat
Healthy

Breakfast

Lunch

Shopping List

Dinner

- [ ]
- [ ]
- [ ]
- [ ]
- [ ]
- [ ]
- [ ]
- [ ]

To Do List

Breakfast

Lunch

Shopping List

Dinner

- [ ]
- [ ]
- [ ]
- [ ]
- [ ]
- [ ]
- [ ]
- [ ]

To Do List

Breakfast

Lunch

Shopping List

Dinner